Major support for Symphony for a Broken Orchestra
was provided by the Pew Center for Arts & Heritage, with additional
support from the Barra Foundation. Temple Contemporary is part of
Tyler School of Art and Architecture at Temple University.

First edition 2022

Library of Congress Catalog Card Number 2021953342
ISBN 978-1-5362-1363-8

22 23 24 25 26 27 APS 10 9 8 7 6 5 4 3 2

Printed in Humen, Dongguan, China

This book was typeset in YWFT Mullino.
The illustrations were created digitally.

Walker Books US
a division of
Candlewick Press
99 Dover Street
Somerville, Massachusetts 02144

www.walkerbooksus.com

SYMPHONY
FOR A BROKEN
ORCHESTRA

How Philadelphia Collected Sounds to Save Music

Amy Ignatow

illustrated by
Gwen Millward

Walker Books

Philadelphia is full of NOISE.
Some noises are LOUD,
and some are soft.

There are sharp noises and dull noises
and funny noises and sad noises.
And music is everywhere in Philadelphia.

We have music in our homes and in our streets and in our grand auditoriums . . .

tika

TIKA

TIKA

Woooooowww

and in our small classrooms where kids get their first instruments so that they can learn to play, too.

And those shiny new saxophones sound great!

They go

WOOOOW

Until the day they don't.

And those snappy new snare drums go

Until they don't.

Does he need to do that right now?
He's practicing to be a mummer.
Well, he definitely sounds like one.
TAK TAK TAK TAK TAK TAK

Waaaa Waa

And those grand new trumpets go

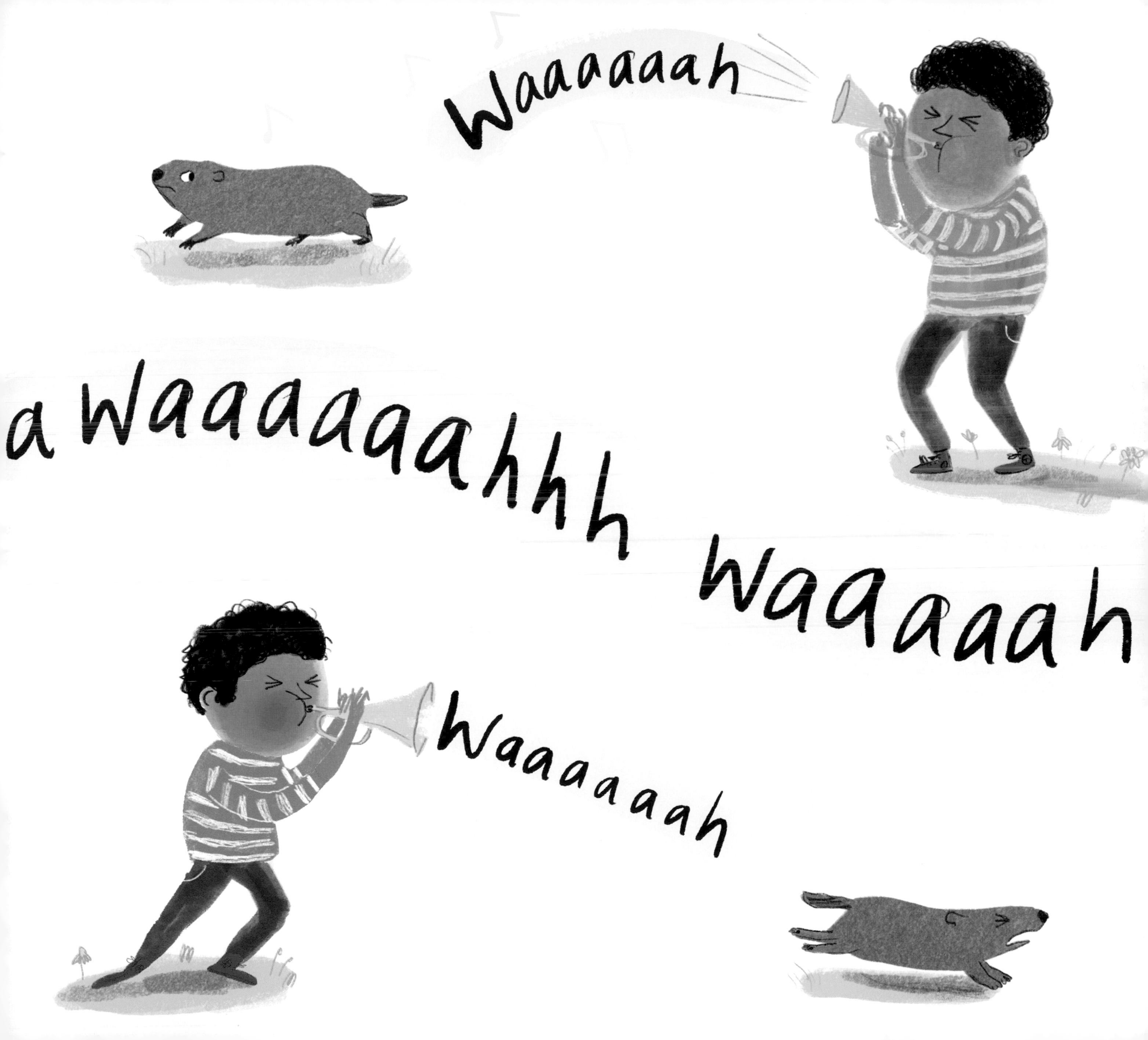
Waaaaaah
aWaaaaaaahhh
Waaaaah
Waaaaaaah

Until they don't.

And those glossy new violins go

Until they don't.

And when the saxophones in Philly can't go
WOOOOOOWWWW
WOOOOOWWWWAAAAHHH
and the snare drums can't go
TiKA tiKA tiKA tiKA tik tik tik tik tik!
and the trumpets can't go
Waaaaaaah waaaawaaaawaacaaahhh
waaaaaaaah
and the violins can't go
Znnnnnn znnnnnnn znnnnnnnzznzzznnnnn . . .

away they go.

And we miss our music.
Because who wants to play a broken instrument?

Our music is more than just the instruments we play.

Because to make music, you need musicians . . .

and Philly has plenty of those!

And musicians will always find a way to make music,
even if it means playing our broken instruments in new and creative ways.
(And fortunately, musicians can be very creative.)

Just because things don't sound
the way that we're used to them sounding
doesn't mean they can't be put together
to make beautiful noise . . .

that gives our
musicians—and their instruments—
another chance to play.

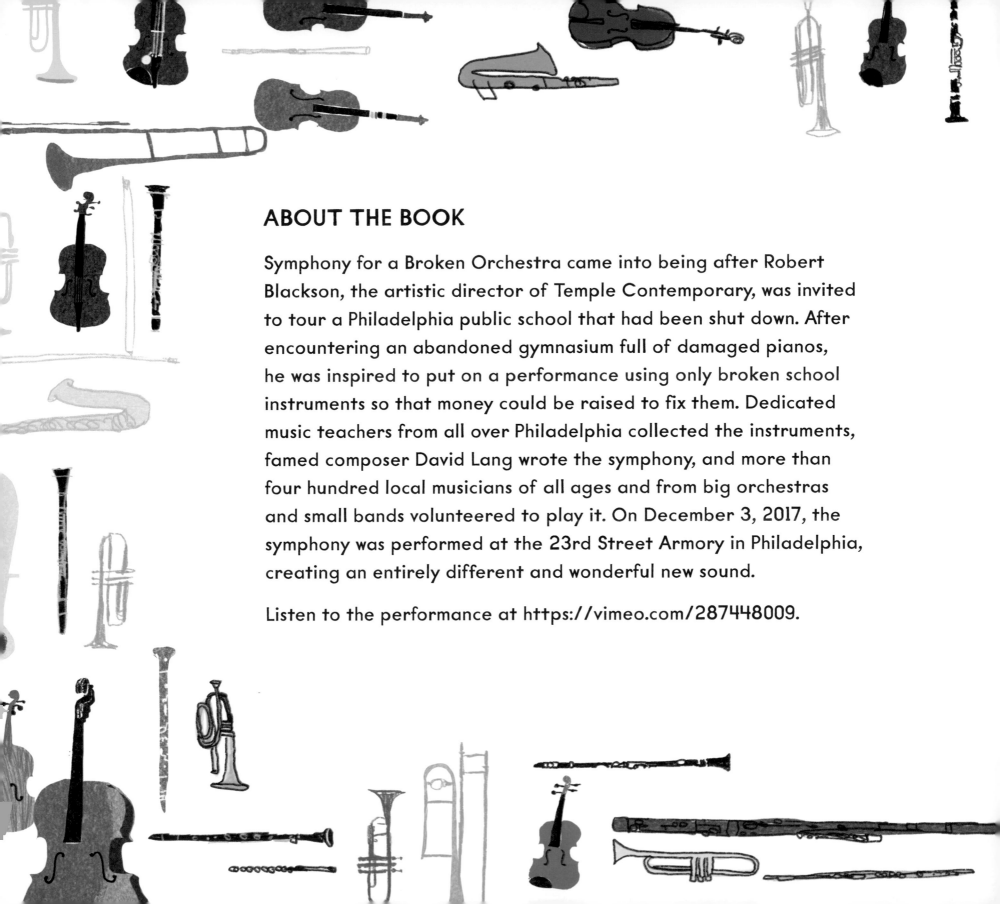

ABOUT THE BOOK

Symphony for a Broken Orchestra came into being after Robert Blackson, the artistic director of Temple Contemporary, was invited to tour a Philadelphia public school that had been shut down. After encountering an abandoned gymnasium full of damaged pianos, he was inspired to put on a performance using only broken school instruments so that money could be raised to fix them. Dedicated music teachers from all over Philadelphia collected the instruments, famed composer David Lang wrote the symphony, and more than four hundred local musicians of all ages and from big orchestras and small bands volunteered to play it. On December 3, 2017, the symphony was performed at the 23rd Street Armory in Philadelphia, creating an entirely different and wonderful new sound.

Listen to the performance at https://vimeo.com/287448009.

A NOTE FROM ROBERT BLACKSON

The success of Symphony for a Broken Orchestra, whose story is lovingly told here by Amy Ignatow with Gwen Millward's beautiful illustrations, was only possible because of musicians and music lovers throughout Philadelphia and beyond.

Thanks to their kindness and generosity, more than one thousand broken musical instruments were repaired and gifted back to Philadelphia schools and put in the hands of children eager to play and learn.

Symphony for a Broken Orchestra is now a nonprofit organization, Broken Orchestra, dedicated to providing music education for all children.

If you would like to be involved with Broken Orchestra or you know of a school that needs our support, please get in touch with our foundation: www.brokenorchestra.org.

Thank you!
Robert Blackson